WE CAN SAVE THE EARTH

THE PEOPLE WE LIVE WITH

Written by:
Jill C. Wheeler

Published by Abdo & Daughters, 6535 Cecilia Circle, Edina, Minnesota 55439.

Library bound edition distributed by Rockbottom Books, Pentagon Tower, P.O. Box 36036, Minneapolis, Minnesota 55435.

Copyright©1991 by Abdo Consulting Group, Inc., Pentagon Tower, P.O. Box 36036, Minneapolis, Minnesota 55435. International copyrights reserved in all countries. No part of this book may be reproduced in any form without written permission from the publisher. Printed in the United States.

Library of Congress Number: 91-073067   ISBN: 1-56239-034-1

Cover Illustrations by: C.A. Nobens
Interiors by: Kristi Schaeppi

Edited by: Stuart Kallen

TABLE OF CONTENTS

Introduction..4

Chapter 1..6
   One Plus One Equals Billions

Chapter 2..9
   How People Affect The Earth

Chapter 3..20
   Why We Grow Like We Do

Chapter 4..24
   Learning To Live Together

Glossary..30

INTRODUCTION

Have you ever gone to a family reunion? Maybe you were surprised at how many aunts, uncles and cousins you had. What would happen if everyone in your neighborhood had a family reunion at the same time? Or if everyone in your town held a family reunion at the same time? That would be a crowd of many, many people.

The world is full of people. More people live on Earth today than ever before – about five billion. If you wanted to eat one cookie for each person on Earth, you would have to eat 95 cookies every minute for 100 years!

As the years pass, it's becoming harder and harder for all five billion people to find enough to eat and drink. It is also becoming more difficult for them to find places to live, to find a place to put the waste they create, to find a job and to find enough energy to support the way they live.

In this book, we will look at what happens when many people live on the same planet. We will also look at what people are doing to help save the Earth for "The People We Live With."

CHAPTER 1

One Plus One Equals Billions

Long ago, there were few people on Earth. These ancient people used primitive tools of wood, stone and bone. They were smarter than the animals they hunted for food so they were able to survive.

As time went on, people learned how to use fire to keep warm. Some moved to colder climates, and the Earth's population began to spread out to different parts of the planet. Some people were killed by the animals they hunted, but others survived and had children. They continued to wander the Earth, searching for food.

About 12,000 years ago, some of the people stopped moving from place to place and began growing crops. These people discovered that farming could produce more food than hunting. Because they had more food, fewer people died of starvation.

Eventually, the people grew more food than they needed to survive. They traded their extra food with other people for goods such as tools and clothing. These items made their lives more comfortable, and they were able to live longer and have more children.

In the late 1700s, the Industrial Revolution began. With it came new inventions such as engines, trains, tractors, harvesting machines and fertilizers. These inventions meant people could move to different places and produce more food. At the same time, people were learning how to control disease. Fewer people became sick and died, and more babies had enough to eat so they could grow up and have children.

Two thousand years ago there were about 200 million people on Earth. It took nearly 1,500 years for that number to double. Today, scientists say the Earth's population will double in less than eighty-five years if current birthrates continue. In some countries, like Mexico, the population is expected to double in the next ten years!

As the Earth's population grows, it's important to look at what more people means to the quality of our environment. In the next chapter, we will see how the growing population is creating a strain on our natural resources.

CHAPTER 2

How People Affect the Earth

The city of Los Angeles used to be a small town. Over the years, people decided they liked the area and moved there. Now, Los Angeles is one of the largest cities in the United States.

Los Angeles used to have plenty of water for its residents. Yet as the city grew, the demand for water also grew. Today, Los Angeles faces a shortage of water because so many people live there.

Shortages of such things as water, food, fuel and shelter are common when an area has more people than it can support. When there is less of something than people want, the price of that product increases. This is called inflation.

Too many people also means there are not enough jobs, so some people cannot earn the money they need to support their families. Without enough money, their standard of living decreases.

But people are not the only ones who suffer from overpopulation. The Earth also suffers.

People change the land they live on more than any other living creature. One person usually only changes the Earth in small ways, resulting in little harm. But multiply those changes by the billions of people and the problem mushrooms.

Our growing population has already caused many changes on Earth. Let's look at some of these.

Deforestation

In many areas of South America, Africa, Central America and Asia, the population is growing so quickly people are running out of space. There is not enough land for everyone to grow crops and raise animals. Without land, the people cannot make money to feed their families.

As the populations in these places have grown, people have started to cut down tropical rain forests so they can use the land for farming. Forests also are cut down to provide cheap paper for industrialized nations, or to create pasture land. The pasture land is used to raise animals for fast-food hamburger restaurants in the United States.

Rain forests make up only 2% of the Earth's surface. But they contain more than half of the world's wild plant, animal and insect species (spee•sheez). Many useful medicines also come from plants found only in our rain forests.

Today, about 50 acres of rain forest is destroyed every minute. Cutting down forests without planting new trees to replace them is called deforestation (dee•for•a•stay•shun). Deforestation kills more than 120 species of plants and animals each day.

Desertification

In North Africa, more people than ever before are trying to graze their cattle on the dry land near the Sahara Desert. They let their cattle roam until the animals have eaten all of the plants in one area. Then the people and their animals go to a different place and do the same thing.

This process leaves the land bare. The soil has no plants to help it hold water, so it dries up and blows away. The area turns into a desert where no plants can grow. This process is called desertification (di•zert•i•fi•kay•shun).

Desertification has caused the Sahara to grow by four million acres each year. That is four million more acres of land that will never produce food for animals or humans again.

Land near deserts is not the only land being harmed because of a growing population. In many parts of the world, land that once was thought unusable for farming now is being farmed because it is the only land available. Land on steep hillsides and land that once supported trees is easily eroded when farmed. Erosion happens when wind and water remove the topsoil. This is the part of the soil that contains the nutrients plants need to grow.

Vanishing Wildlife

People throughout the world are clearing land that once supported wildlife. As people turn the forests into fields and build homes there, the animals must go somewhere else. Often there is nowhere else to go, and the animals are either killed by people or die of starvation.

The Earth is now losing up to three species of animals each day. By the year 2000, a full twenty percent of the world's animal species may be gone forever.

Dwindling Seas

In the 1950s, people looked to the sea to help feed the growing population. New technology enabled people to catch more fish than ever before. By the 1970s, the number of fish caught had begun to drop and some species were becoming less common.

Scientists realized people had caught the fish faster than the fish could reproduce. Today, many sea animals like whales and dolphins are threatened with extinction because people have killed too many of them.

Fish and marine animals also are threatened by water pollution. Many deadly poisons from sewage plants, farm fields, oil refineries and factories are being dumped into the sea, where they kill marine life.

Dirty Air, Dirty Water

More people also means more of every kind of pollution. As more people live on the Earth, they produce more garbage. This is burned, dumped into the oceans, or buried in landfills. Burning garbage pollutes the air. Dumping it in oceans pollutes the water. Landfills take up space and pollute the water in the ground below them.

More people means more pesticides and herbicides must be used to make the land produce more food. These chemicals run off the fields and into drinking water and make some people sick. Factories that make these chemicals also pollute the air and water.

More people means more factories are needed to produce goods to keep everyone happy. These factories often pollute the air and water. They require energy to operate. This energy is usually supplied by burning fossil fuels such as coal and oil. Fossil fuels cannot be replaced once they have been used up. The burning of fossil fuels produces air pollution and leads to acid rain. Acid rain kills plants and fish.

The burning of fossil fuels may also be causing the Earth's overall temperature to rise. This is called the greenhouse effect. The greenhouse effect changes weather patterns, sending more rain to some areas and less to others. Food-producing areas that get less rain because of the greenhouse effect may turn into deserts.

More people means there are more cars producing carbon dioxide, primarily in developed nations. Carbon dioxide harms the Earth's protective ozone layer. This means more harmful ultraviolet radiation from the sun reaches people and makes them sick.

We have seen that a growing population causes many problems. In the next chapter, we will look at why populations grow the way they do.

Did You Know...
- In 1951, there were six cities in the world which had more than five million residents. By the year 2000, scientists predict there will be 60.

- About one-third of the people on Earth are under 15 years of age.

- In India, the average house has two rooms. In the United States, the average house has five rooms.

CHAPTER 3

Why We Grow Like We Do

History has shown that populations tend to grow when times are good and people have the food, money and work they need. But then the population grows too much and people suffer.

If too many people make life harder for everyone, then why do populations grow? There are many reasons.

Americans used to be encouraged to have large families. For example, in 1800, the average American woman had seven children. At that time, most people were farmers and much of the work was done by hand. Children were needed to help with the work so everyone could be fed.

There also was more disease at that time. Families knew that all of their children might not live to be adults, so they had large families in hopes that some children would survive.

Today, the average American woman has about two children. American families no longer require many children because machines do much of the work. Also, many of the diseases which used to kill children, such as smallpox and diphtheria, now are under control.

In underdeveloped, or Third World, countries, people have few machines to do the work. They still depend on many hands. Many of these countries also have poor sanitation and impure drinking water. These problems cause disease to spread and kill thousands of children each year.

In addition, unlike most people in developed nations, Third World residents have not been educated on how to limit the size of their families. Many are also discouraged from having smaller families by their governments, their culture, or their religious beliefs.

The way people in a country view women also plays a role in population growth. In some countries, women are limited to their homes and children. For these women, more children means more respect. In other countries, women are not given a choice of how many children they have.

These women often die at a young age because their bodies cannot survive the strain of having so many babies.

Differing views on family size have created many conflicts between nations. People in developed countries question why people in Third World countries have so many children. They ask why Third World residents have more children when their families are already poor.

Families in Third World countries ask why the small number of people in developed nations use so many of the Earth's resources. The United States contains only five percent of the world's population, yet U.S. residents use twenty percent of the Earth's resources. People in the Third World want to live as well as Americans, but the Earth does not contain enough resources for everyone to live this way.

People around the world continue to struggle with these and other questions. There are no clear answers. But people are learning how to live together and share the Earth. The next chapter looks at some of the things they're doing.

CHAPTER 4

Learning to Live Together

Many people around the world have realized the dangers of too many people. Together with the governments of their countries, these people are working to save the Earth.

These are some of the things that they are doing:

- Population Control – Some governments are encouraging families to have fewer children than before. Couples who limit their families to one child receive special treatment. China is one nation which has been able to curb its population growth this way.

Some social changes also contribute to population control. Fewer diseases, better sanitation, a higher status for women, and better education all lead to smaller families.

- Soil Conservation – Farmers around the world are learning to use soil conservation techniques to protect their topsoil. Soil conservation techniques include using terraces, which look like giant steps down a hillside. Because the land on the terraces is flat, instead of sloped (like before), the topsoil does not wash off as easily.

- Organic Farming – Some farmers have stopped using pesticides and herbicides in favor of natural fertilizers like animal dung. Less herbicides and pesticides mean less water pollution, and the energy used to make those chemicals is saved.

- Energy Conservation – The less energy each person uses, the more energy will be available for the rest of the world. Energy conservation can be done many ways. For example, people save energy and reduce highway congestion by riding with other people in a car-pool. Many people ride public transportation such as buses and trains. People also save energy by recycling trash instead of throwing it away. Recycling an aluminium can takes just four percent of the energy needed to make it from scratch.

- Alternative Energy – Fossil fuels are not the only source of energy on the Earth. There is energy in the sun, the wind and the water. Technology is improving solar collectors, windmills and water turbines to harness this energy. All of these energy sources are renewable, so we will never use them up.
- Saving the Rain Forests – Many people are working to save the rain forests from destruction. They are encouraging people to earn money by using the products that the rain forests already produce. This is better than cutting the forests down for farming. Some governments have also promised to protect some areas of rain forest from destruction.

It is easy to blame the problem of overpopulation on other people. But we are all responsible for the damage now being done to the Earth.

And we all can do something about it, by recycling, saving energy and learning more about the world around us. The time to start is today!

GLOSSARY

AGRICULTURE – The work of growing plants and raising animals for food.

BIRTHRATE – The number of live babies born per 1,000 people per year.

EROSION – The wearing away of soil or rock by wind and water.

DEFORESTATION – Clearing land of trees.

DESERTIFICATION – When an area of land becomes desert through climate change, over-grazing or over-farming.

FOSSIL FUELS – Fuels produced by the remains of prehistoric plants and organisms. They include oil, coal and natural gas.

HERBICIDES – Chemical poisons used to kill weeds.

INDUSTRIAL REVOLUTION – When society changed from farm-based to industry-based during the 1700s. The Industrial Revolution resulted from the invention of new machines and factories.

INSECTICIDES – Chemical poisons used to kill unwanted insects.

OZONE – A form of oxygen found high in the atmosphere. It protects us from most of the sun's ultraviolet radiation.

POLLUTION – The poisoning or dirtying of air, land or water by impurities.

RAIN FOREST – Forest found in rainy climates. Tropical rain forests have more plant and animal species than any other kind of place.

SOIL – Particles of rock mixed with decayed plant and animal matter. Soil provides plants with a roothold and nourishment.

SPECIES – The smallest grouping of related plants or animals.

THIRD WORLD – A name often used for the world's poor nations, located primarily in the tropics in Asia, Central America, South America and Africa.